BIBLE PEOPLE BOOK THREE

(Prophets and Writings)

A Workbook By Joel Lurie Grishaver

Alternatives in Religious Education, Inc.

Welcome to *Bible People Book Three*.

In this workbook, the adventure continues. This time we meet a new generation of Bible People. Like you, these people also studied the lives of the earlier Bible people. They used what they learned to turn the land of Canaan into a Jewish country called Israel.

At the end of *Bible People Book Two*, we finished the book of Deuteronomy which is the end of the Torah.

The Torah is the first of the three sections of the Bible. We know that the Torah is sometimes printed into a book and sometimes handwritten on a scroll. The Torah is made up of five books. Can you remember the order in which they go?

_____ Leviticus

_____ Genesis

_____ Deuteronomy

_____ Exodus

_____ Numbers

The Hebrew Bible is called Tanach from the first letters of its three sections:

The 5 Books of the Torah

The Books of the Prophets

The Books of the Writings

Torah	ת	Torah
Nevi-im	נ	Prophets
Ketuv-im	ך	Writings

Now our story continues.

For forty years, the Jewish people lived in the desert. They had only measured amounts of water to drink and little to eat besides the manna which they gathered every morning. Life was difficult.

During those forty years in the desert, the Jewish people were led by these three great leaders. By the end of the book of Deuteronomy, all of them had died. Joshua then became the leader of the Children of Israel.

It was up to Joshua to lead the Jewish people into the land of Canaan. Under his leadership, the Jewish people conquered and settled this land and made it into a Jewish country. Here the books of the Prophets begin and our stories continue.

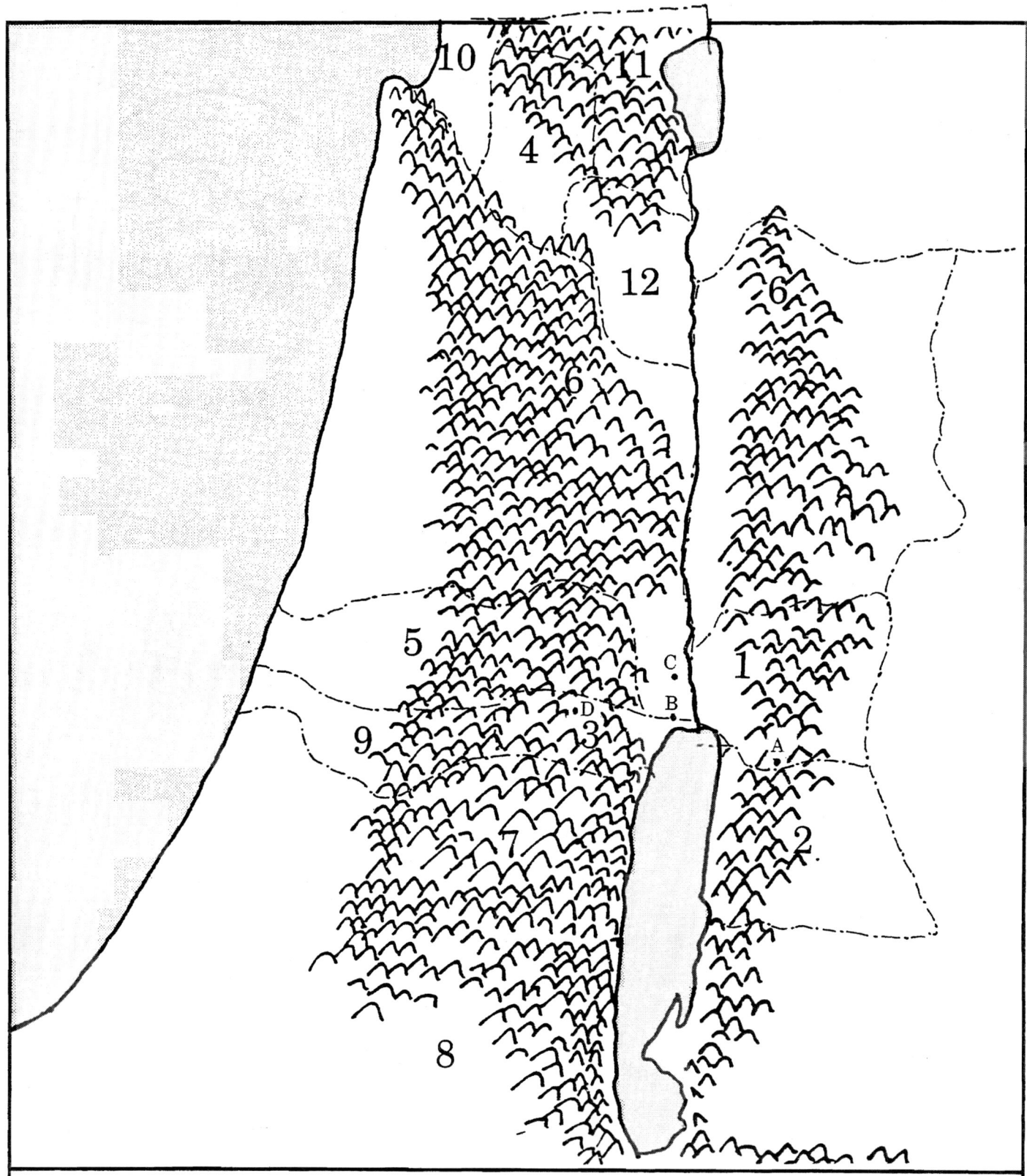

Before the children of Israel could enter the land of Canaan, Joshua sent in some spies. Do you remember what happened when Moses sent spies into the land?

If you were a spy, would you remember where these places are? Place them on the map.

| The Jordan River | The Sea of Galilee | The Coastal Plain | The Judean Hills |
| The Dead Sea | The Negev | The Great Sea | |

Write in the names of these places next to the the letters on the map:

A. Mt. Nebo B. Gilgal C. Jericho D. Ai

JOSHUA

Be strong and resolute; Do not be terrified or dismayed, for the Lord your God is with you wherever you go.

Joshua 1:9

Becoming/Being a Leader

Which of these things did Joshua do when he was training under Moses to lead the Jewish people? Which did he do when he was leading the Jewish people after Moses' death? Mark T in the box for training and L in the box for leading.

- Studied Torah with Moses
- Went on a spy mission
- Watched Moses judge
- Led the people in conquering the land
- Led the people in battling Amalek
- Taught Torah to the people
- Watched Moses talk with God
- Received messages from God
- Sent out spies
- Divided up the land fairly among the tribes

Can you match things Joshua learned during training with things Joshua did as a leader?

                Training   Leading

1 _____   _____

2 _____   _____

3 _____   _____

4 _____   _____

5 _____   _____

When Moses died, God said: THERE WILL NEVER AGAIN ARISE ANOTHER PROPHET LIKE MOSES.

Then God said to Joshua: I WILL BE WITH YOU AS I WAS WITH MOSES.

List some things which Moses did better than Joshua.	List some things both Moses and Joshua did equally well.	List some things which Joshua did better than Moses.
_____	_____	_____
_____	_____	_____
_____	_____	_____
_____	_____	_____
_____	_____	_____
_____	_____	_____

We know that people are always being compared to others. Joshua was compared to Moses. You have probably been compared to others, too.

List three people with whom you have been compared.

_____ _____ _____

List three people you'd like to be like.

_____ _____ _____

List three things you do better than those with whom you are compared.

_____ _____ _____

List three things you don't do as well as those with whom you are compared.

_____ _____ _____

1. A good thing about being compared is _____

_____

2. A problem with being compared is _____

_____

Imagine that you were an instant news reporter back in the days when Israel conquered Jericho. You are given a chance to interview Rahab. Complete this interview by filling in the blanks or by circling the answers Rahab really gave.

1. Where did you first meet the two Israelite spies?

They came to me. I have this house where I take in guests. They came looking for a place to lodge. My house was located in the _____ of Jericho.

2. Why did you decide to help them?

    a. One of them was really cute and I sort of fell in love with him.

    b. I knew what the King would do to them, and I didn't want anyone to be tortured and killed.

    c. I knew that God had already helped the Jews, and that soon they would conquer Canaan. I wanted to be on the surviving side.

3. So how did you help them?

   When the King's men came looking for spies, I told them, "The men were here but they _____."
   Then I hid the two men under some straw on my _____.

4. You spoke to them while they were hiding. What did you talk about?

   a. I gave them all kinds of information about the city and its weak points. We talked about the guards and the walls.

   b. We talked about little things. We talked about our families, about our lives and so on. We made small talk.

   c. We talked about God. They told me all about the Jewish religion and the laws which God had given to Israel in the Torah.

5. You worked out a promise with the Israelites. Can you tell us the conditions of the oath you made them swear?

   They said that they would protect _____

   if I _____ from my window.

6. Rahab, now that Jericho has been destroyed, what do you think you will do?

   a. I think that I will leave Canaan, and try to build a new life somewhere else. If I stay here, I am afraid that people will find out what I did.

   b. I think that I will move to Ai or Hebron, or one of the near by cities in Canaan, and reestablish my house.

   c. I am going to convert and become a Jew, because their God is a powerful God, and has much to teach all people about the meaning of life.

Rahab is one of many non-Jews in the Bible. Describe how each of these people treated the Jews:

HAGAR _____

JOSEPH'S PHARAOH _____

JETHRO _____

PHARAOH'S DAUGHTER _____

MOSES' PHARAOH _____

BALAAM _____

BALAK _____

HAMAN _____

Mark each of these statements true or false.

_____ Most Jews are rich.
_____ There are almost no poor Jews.
_____ Most Jews are smart (and do well in school).
_____ Jews tend to take care of other Jews.
_____ Jews should have mainly Jewish friends.
_____ Judaism is the best religion.
_____ All religions are equally good.
_____ Most non-Jews hate Jews.
_____ The non-Jewish world will never totally accept Jews.
_____ Jews should only marry Jews.

Deborah, wife of Lappidoth, was a prophetess; she led Israel at that time. She used to sit under the Palm of Deborah, between Ramah and Bethel...and the Israelites would come to her for decisions.

Judges 4:4-5

In order to understand the book of Deborah, you need to know where the tribes settled. Go back to the map on page 6, and write in the name of each tribe in their territory. Use the numbers to help you.

1. Gad	4. Zebulun	7. Manasseh	10. Asher
2. Reuben	5. Ephraim	8. Simeon	11. Naphtali
3. Benjamin	6. Judah	9. Dan	12. Issachar

In the book of Judges, Deborah and Barak sing a song about their victory. From that song we learn a lot about what really happened. Read these two small sections of the song and answer the questions which follow.

> In the days of Shamgar son of Anath
> In the days of Jael, caravans stopped
> And travelers went
> By roundabout paths.
> Deliverance ceased,
> Ceased in Israel....

1. Why did the Israelites need to go to war? What were the Canaanites doing to them?

_____

_____

> From **Ephraim** came they whose roots are in Amalek:
> After you, your kin **Benjamin;**
> From Machir (**Manasseh**) came down leaders,
> From **Zebulun** those who carried the marshals staff.
> And **Issachar's** chiefs were with Deborah;
> And Barak's tribe (**Naphtali**), too.
>
> Among the clans of **Reuben**
> Were great searchings of heart...
> Gilead (**Gad**) tarried beyond the Jordan;
> And **Dan** – why did he linger by the ships?
> **Asher** remained at the seacoast.
> And tarried at his landings.

2. How many tribes joined with Deborah and Barak? _____

3. How many tribes do we know didn't join in? _____

4. Which tribes aren't mentioned? _____

5. Turn back to the map on page 6. Color all the tribes who came to fight in red. Color all those who the song tells us didn't fight in blue. Color those which are not mentioned in green.

   What does the geography tell you about which tribes did and did not join Deborah and Barak and about those which aren't mentioned?

   _____

   _____

6. How unified do you think the various tribes were at this time?

   _____

REASONS FOR FIGHTING

Deborah was a judge. When the Canaanites cut off trade, she decided that it was a reason for going to war. Circle the phrases below which give you good enough reason to get into a fight (not just a little pushing and shoving on the playground, but a real fight in which someone could get hurt or even killed). If there are no good reasons for fighting, then circle number 10.

1. Someone attacks you.
2. Someone calls your mother a name.
3. Someone spray paints bad things about Jews on a wall.
4. Someone calls you a "chicken."
5. Someone is stealing from you.
6. Someone is hurting another person.
7. Someone spits in your face.
8. Someone won't let you pass.
9. Someone won't let another person pass.
10. There are no good reasons for fighting.

Circle the phrases below which give a country or group of people good enough reason to go to war. If there are no good reasons to go to war, then circle number 10.

1. To protect your own freedom
2. To spread a religion or idea
3. To create a Jewish homeland
4. To expand a country
5. To protect freedom of others
6. To defend yourself from attack
7. To defend others from attack
8. To rule a country
9. To remain in power
10. There is no good reason for going to war.

17

JUDAISM AND FIGHTING

The Rabbis of the *Talmud* didn't like war or fighting, but they understood that sometimes violence was necessary. They thought and wrote about fighting and fighting back. Here are a few of the Rabbis' thoughts about fighting and going to war.

If person A sees person B chasing person C – to kill or assualt person C – then person A is obligated to kill person B if necessary in order to prevent person B from completing this sin.

(Sanhedrin)

If a person is found breaking into a home, the owner may kill the burglar, because it is assumed that the burglar would kill those who discovered his breaking in.

(Sanhedrin)

There are two kinds of wars. The king does not need permission from the Sanhedrin (court) to fight a *mitzvah* (command) war. He does, however, need permission from the Sanhedrin to fight an optional war.

MITZVAH WARS

- A war to take the land of Israel
- A war to defeat Amalek (a totally evil nation)
- A war to defend Israel

OPTIONAL WARS

- A war against nations not living in Israel
- A war to extend the borders of Israel
- A war to become more powerful

Underline the incidents on page 19 which you think the Rabbis would have accepted as reasons for fighting back or going to war.

SAMSON

You are going to conceive and bear a son; let no razor touch his head, for the boy is to be a Nazirite to God from the womb on. He shall be the first to deliver Israel from the Philistines.

Judges 13:5

We know that Samson was very strong physically, but that he was very weak when relating to Delilah. Everyone has strengths and weaknesses.

List five strengths you feel you have, and five weaknesses which you also have:

Strengths	Weaknesses
1. _____	_____
2. _____	_____
3. _____	_____
4. _____	_____
5. _____	_____

List two problems which your strengths create and two good things which happen because of your weaknesses.

1. _____
2. _____

1. _____
2. _____

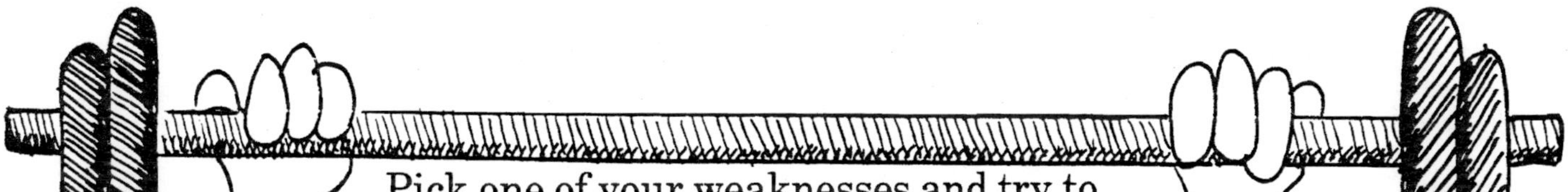

Pick one of your weaknesses and try to change it to a stength. Pick a partner to help you with this. Meet once a week, and report to each other how your "work" on weaknesses is going.

WHO IS WISE?

In *Pirke Avot*, the Rabbis discuss wisdom, strength, wealth and honor. Ben Zoma said:

Who is wise?	Who is strong?
 One who learns from every person.	One who conquers his/her impulses.
Who is rich?	**Who is honored?**
One who is content with his/her portion.	One who honors all people.

Do as the Rabbis did. Write your own creative definitions of wisdom, strength, wealth and honor.

1. Who is wise? _____

2. Who is strong? _____

3. Who is rich? _____

4. Who is honored? _____

The word *chesed* appears over and over again in the book of Ruth. It is usually translated as "loving kindness," but it means acting with real care and concern for another person. Give one example of how each of these Bible people acted with *chesed*.

ORPAH	RUTH	NAOMI

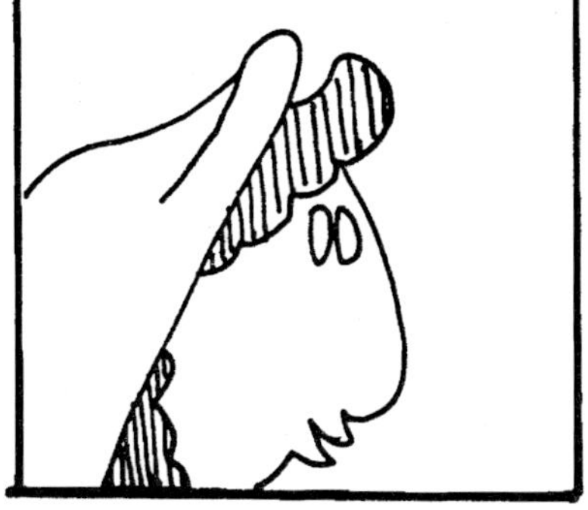

BOAZ	YOU

This corner is reserved for the widow, the orphan, and the poor.

Naomi was a Jew by birth. Ruth became a Jew by choice. People who become Jews are called converts. If you were going to help teach converts, think about what experiences you would want them to have.

What three things would you want them to know?

1. _____
2. _____
3. _____

What three things would you want them to know how to do?

1. _____
2. _____
3. _____

What three things would you want them to believe?

1. _____
2. _____
3. _____

What ceremonies do you think that they should go through?

1. _____
2. _____

Standing in the Chain

At the end of the book of Ruth, Ruth marries Boaz. We are told that they had a son named Obed. Obed had a son named Jesse, and Jesse had a number of sons, including King David. You might think that it was strange that the most important of all Israel's kings was descended from a convert. What do you think David might have inherited from Ruth?

Fill out this side in class.

1. What does your family name mean?

2. What does you family name stand for?

3. What is the most important thing or quality you received from your parents?

4. What do you think is the most important thing your parents learned from your grandparents?

5. What do you think is the most significant thing you will eventually have which was your parents?

6. What do you think is the most important thing you will learn from your parents?

Interview one of your parents and fill out this side.

1. What does our family name mean?

2. What does our family name stand for?

3. What is the most important thing or quality we received from your parents?

4. What do you think is the most important thing you learned from your parents?

5. What of yours do you think will be most important to me when I eventually own it?

6. What one thing do you most want me to learn from you?

"Young Samuel grew up in the service of the Lord."
I Samuel 2:21

THIS IS YOUR LIFE: SAMUEL

Put the things these people remember in the right order to tell the life story of Samuel.

☐ Samuel was a good leader. However, the people wanted a King. Samuel decided that I was the right person and he annointed me the first king of Israel.
— KING SAUL

☐ I remember that I had two wives: Peninnah and Hannah. Peninnah had lots of children, but Hannah didn't have any.
— ELKANAH - A MAN FROM EPHRAIM

☐ Eli's sons were evil. Once they took the Ark into a battle. They were both killed and the Ark was lost to the Philistines. When he heard the news, Eli died and Samuel became the new High Priest.
— A PERSON OF ISRAEL.

☐ I remember that I found a woman praying in the Sanctuary because she wanted to have a son. When the son was born, she brought him to me, to dedicate his life to God.
— ELI - THE HIGH PRIEST

☐ I remember that one night while Samuel was with Eli, God called to him. At first Samuel thought it was Eli calling, but later he realized that it was God.
— HANNAH SAMUEL'S MOTHER

☐ When Samuel decided that the Jewish people needed a new king, he chose me.
— KING DAVID

HINENI is one of the big words in Samuel's life. It is the answer that he gives God when he is first called. It means more than "I am here." It also means "I am willing and I am ready."

Abraham says HINENI three times in the story of the binding of Isaac.	

When Moses is at the Burning Bush, HINENI is his response.	

When he realized that Abraham, Moses and Samuel all say HINENI, Rashi (a famous biblical commentator) said that HINENI is the response the righteous person gives when called.

List three things in today's world to which Jews need to say HINENI.

1. _____

2. _____

3. _____

The bow of Jonathan never turned back;
The sword of Saul never withdrew empty.

II Samuel 1:22

Which of these things happened to Saul? Which happened to Jonathan? Which happened to both of them? Write S for Saul and J for Jonathan and B for Both.

_____ Goes looking for his father's donkeys

_____ Was anointed king by Samuel

_____ Spoke like a prophet in ecstacy

_____ Defended the people of Jabesh-gilead

_____ Was made king by the people

_____ Fought the Philistines

_____ Ate honey and fought on a day when no one was supposed to eat

_____ Got Samuel angry

_____ Had David play the harp

_____ Was David's best friend

_____ Tried to kill David

_____ Saved David's life

_____ Died in battle

SAUL | JONATHAN

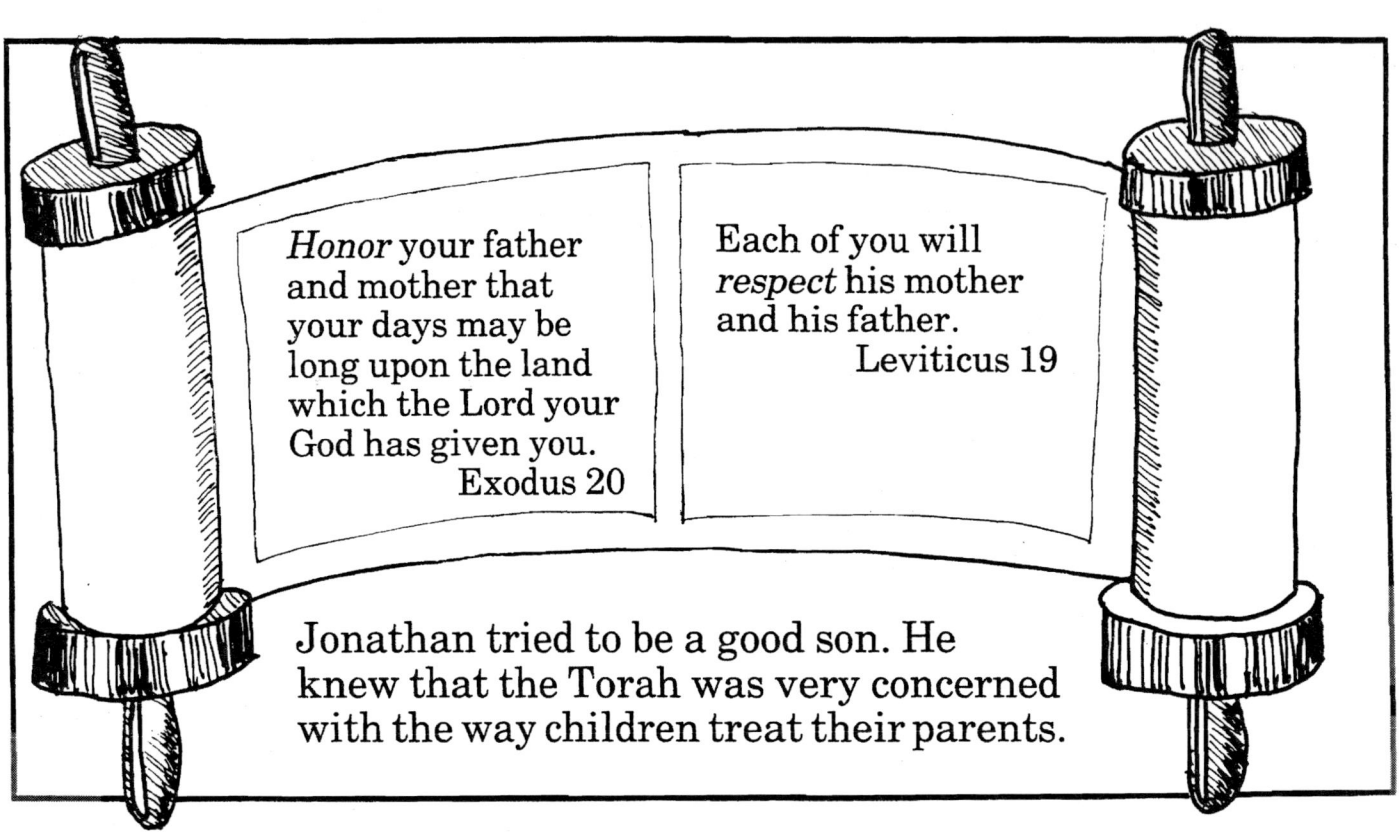

Honor your father and mother that your days may be long upon the land which the Lord your God has given you.
Exodus 20

Each of you will *respect* his mother and his father.
Leviticus 19

Jonathan tried to be a good son. He knew that the Torah was very concerned with the way children treat their parents.

Draw and describe three ways of honoring parents:

Draw and describe three ways of respecting parents:

What do you think the difference is between honoring and respecting?
_____
_____

Jonathan and David were best friends. The Bible says: Jonathan loved David as he loved himself.

Being a friend is something special. A Chasidic Rabbi, Moshe Leib of Sasov, told a story of how he learned about love from two Russian peasants in a bar:

Think about your best friend. Can you think of a time that your best friend understood what was bothering you? Was there a time that you understood what was bothering your best friend?

_____

_____

Explain why Moshe Leib says that one who knows what gives his friend pain is indeed a good friend.

Jonathan had a problem. He was caught between his love for his father and his friendship for David

Have you ever had to decide between doing what your parents think is right and doing what your friends think is best?

Write about a time like this:

_____
_____
_____
_____
_____
_____
_____
_____

How did Jonathan solve his problem?
_____

How did you solve your problem?
_____

David was beautiful to look at – like a rose among the thorns.
                                               Folk Saying

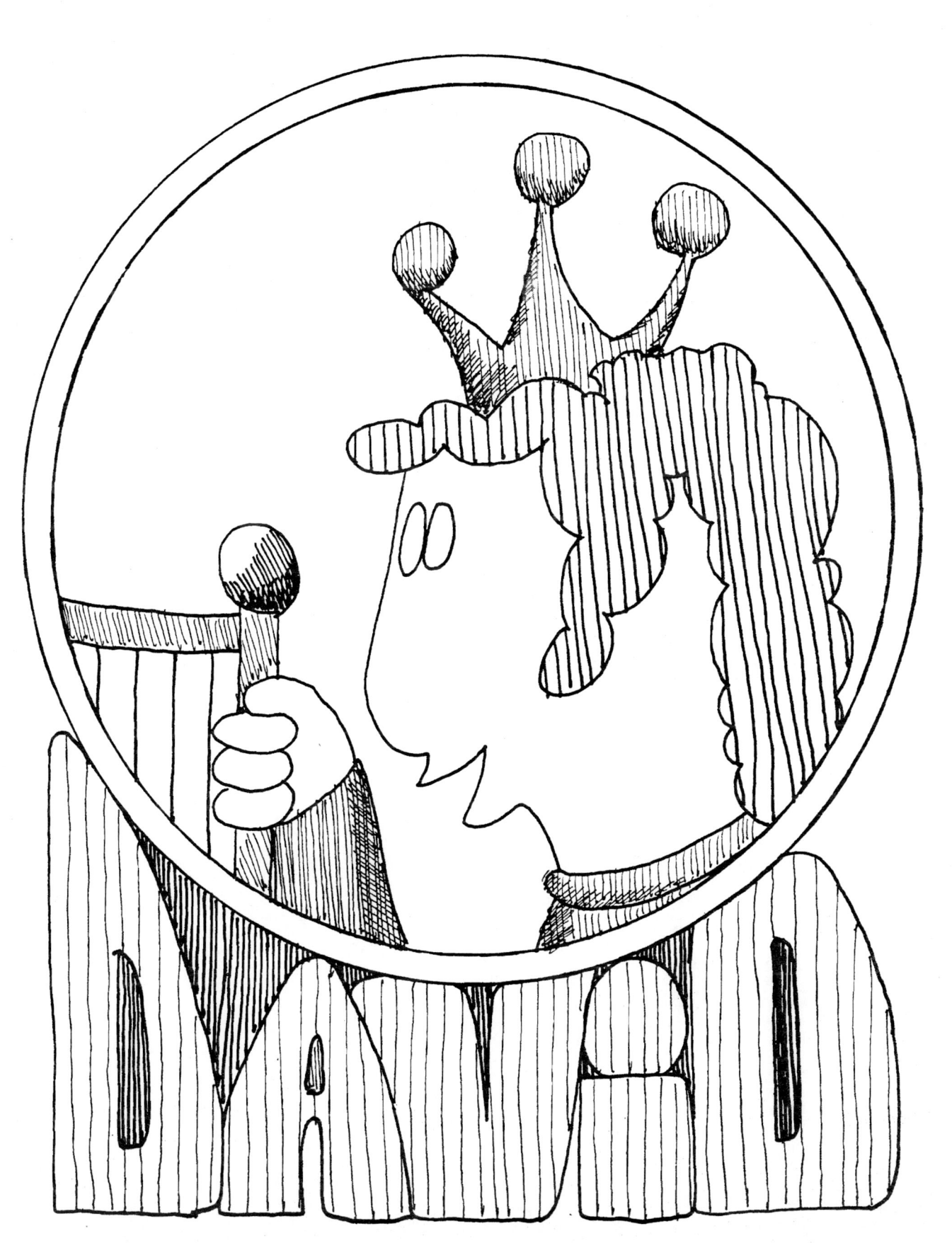

THE CAST OF THE DAVID STORY

The story of David is the longest and most exciting single story in the Torah. It has lots of characters. Complete these cards of the David story by pasting the description (on page 41) onto the correct card.

Michal	Jesse	Samuel

Saul	Jonathan	Ruth

Nathan	Abner	Mephiboshet
Bathsheva	Ish Boshet	Abigail

Ahimelech	Joash	Absalom
King David's father	Saul's son who was David's best friend	The first king of Israel who befriended David, then tried to kill him
Saul's General who at first backed Saul's son Ish Boshet for king, but later supported David. He was murdered	A Philistine woman who helped David and who later married him	Saul's daughter who became David's wife
A prophet who frequents David's court	Jonathan's crippled son, for whom David cares	David's son who kills his half brother Amnon. (Amnon had seduced his sister.) Later he rebels against his father and tries to take the throne.
Priest of Nob who befriended David	A woman David stole from Uriah the Hittite and then marries Solomon's mother	Saul's son who was David's rival for king after Saul and Jonathan are dead
King David's great grandmother (a Moabite convert to Judaism)	The High Priest who was a prophet. He anointed both Saul and David	David's general

KING DAVID'S RESUME

King David held lots of jobs during his lifetime. Imagine what would happen if he had to apply for another job. Fill in the information on this resume.

SHEPHERD

Place _____ Time _____ Reference _____

HERO

Place _____ Time _____ Reference _____

SOLDIER

Place _____ Time _____ Reference _____

MUSICIAN

Place _____ Time _____ Reference _____

KING

Place _____ Time _____ Reference _____

POET

Place _____ Time _____ Reference _____

HUNTED CRIMINAL

Place _____ Time _____ Reference _____

If you had to apply for a job, what experiences could you list?

Job _____ Place _____ Time _____ Reference _____

Job _____ Place _____ Time _____ Reference _____

Job _____ Place _____ Time _____ Reference _____

DISAPPOINMENT

King David's life didn't exactly go the way he wanted it to. He had to deal with many disappointments. Number these events in the order you think that they bothered David. Number one should be the thing which you think bothered David the most.

His king tries to kill him _____

He becomes an outlaw in his own land _____

His son dies _____

His son tries to steal his throne _____

His best friend is killed _____

His wife, for whom he waited years to marry, rejected him _____

Nathan tells him that marrying Bathsheva was wrong _____

God won't let him build the Temple _____

List five disappointments with which you have had to deal. Then number them in order from the hardest to deal with (#1) to the least hard (# 5).

____ _____

____ _____

____ _____

____ _____

____ _____

PSALM 23

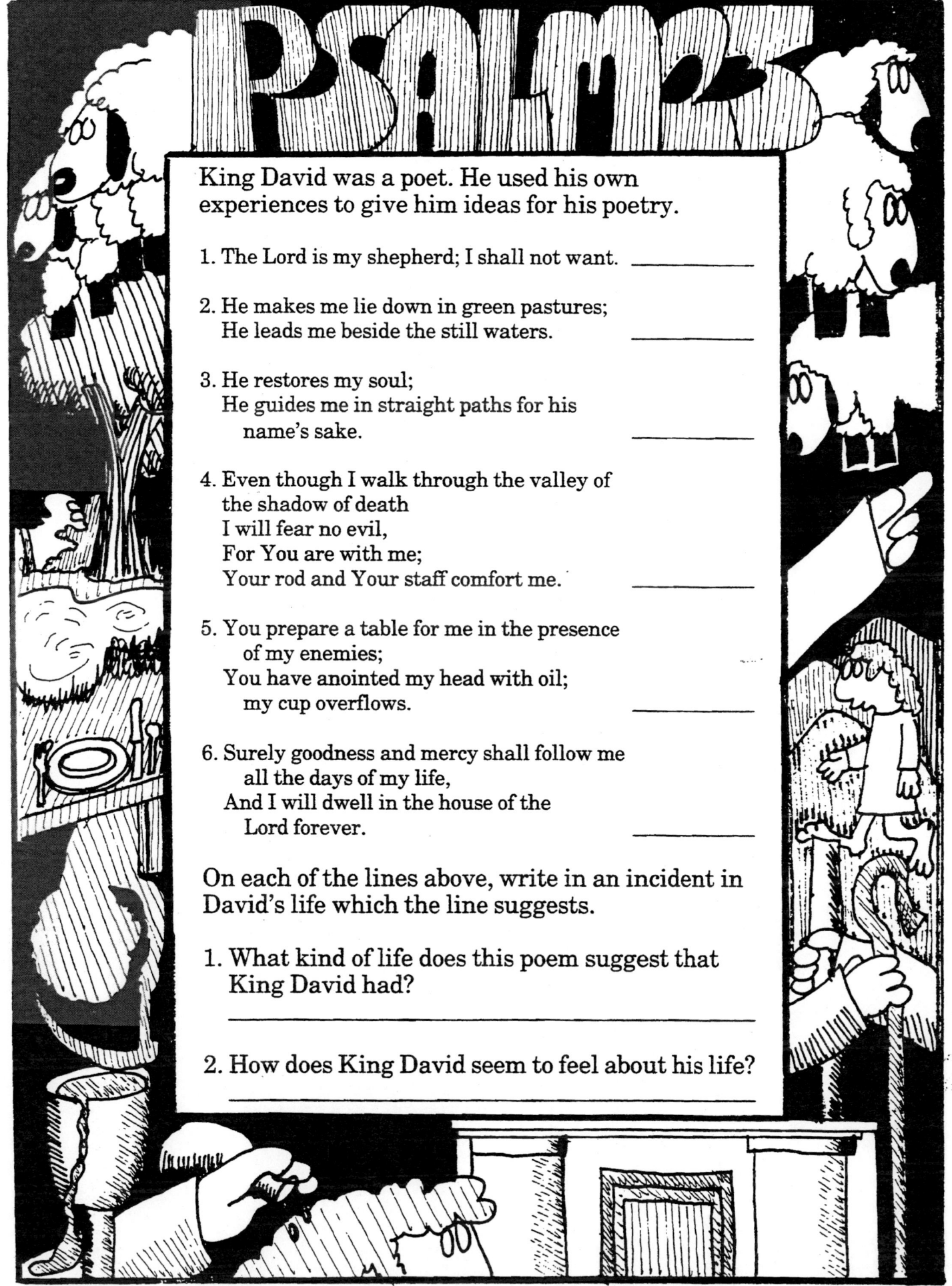

King David was a poet. He used his own experiences to give him ideas for his poetry.

1. The Lord is my shepherd; I shall not want. _____

2. He makes me lie down in green pastures;
   He leads me beside the still waters. _____

3. He restores my soul;
   He guides me in straight paths for his
      name's sake. _____

4. Even though I walk through the valley of
      the shadow of death
   I will fear no evil,
   For You are with me;
   Your rod and Your staff comfort me. _____

5. You prepare a table for me in the presence
      of my enemies;
   You have anointed my head with oil;
      my cup overflows. _____

6. Surely goodness and mercy shall follow me
      all the days of my life,
   And I will dwell in the house of the
      Lord forever. _____

On each of the lines above, write in an incident in David's life which the line suggests.

1. What kind of life does this poem suggest that King David had?
   _____

2. How does King David seem to feel about his life?
   _____

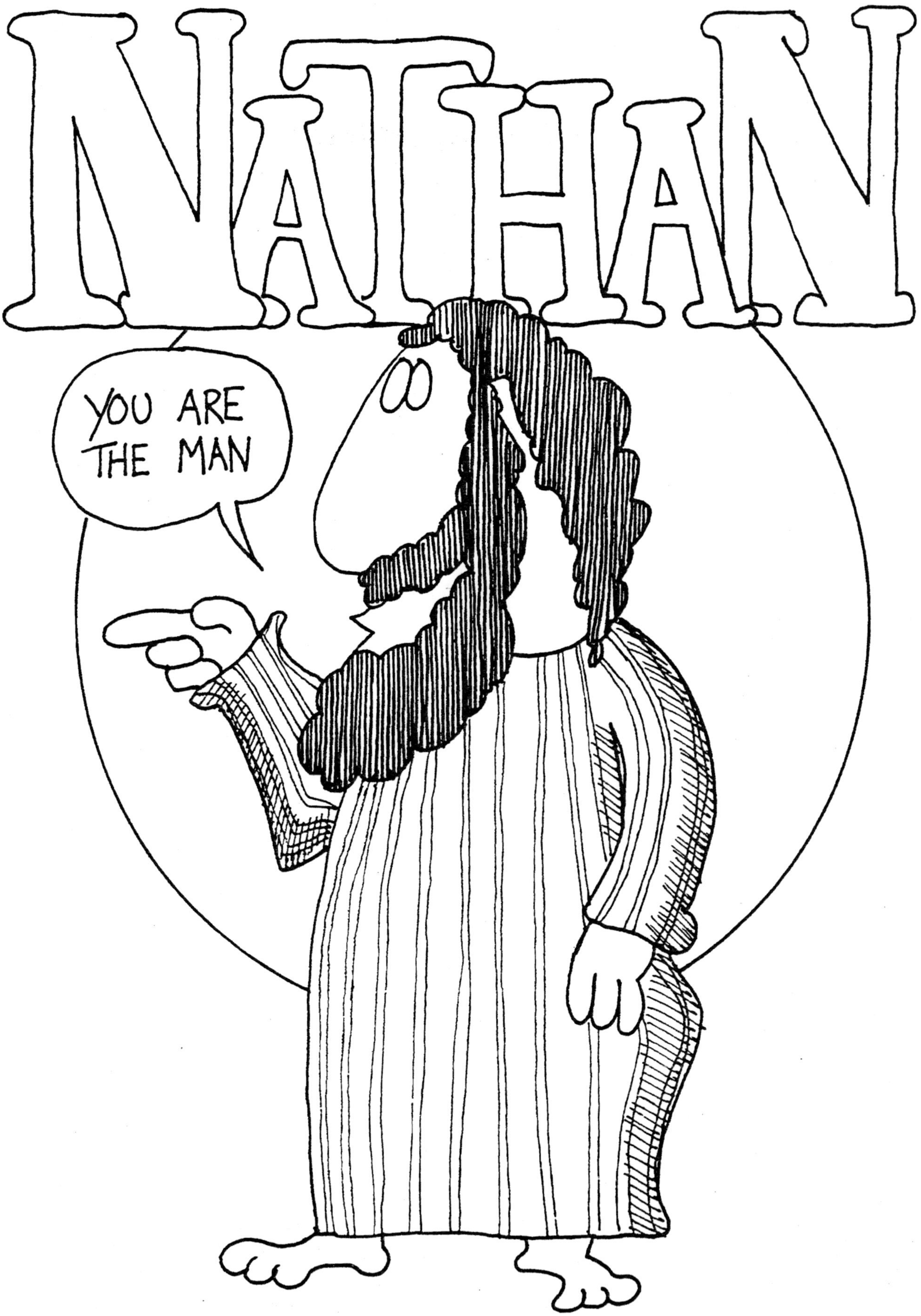
NATHAN
YOU ARE THE MAN

Nathan used a parable (II Samuel 12:1-7) to tell King David what he was doing wrong.

Who did each character in Nathan's parable represent?

THE RICH MAN

THE SHEEP

THE POOR MAN

With what other words or actions might Nathan have shown he was displeased with King David's actions?

Now that you have been working with a parable, can you explain what a parable is?

SPEAKING UP

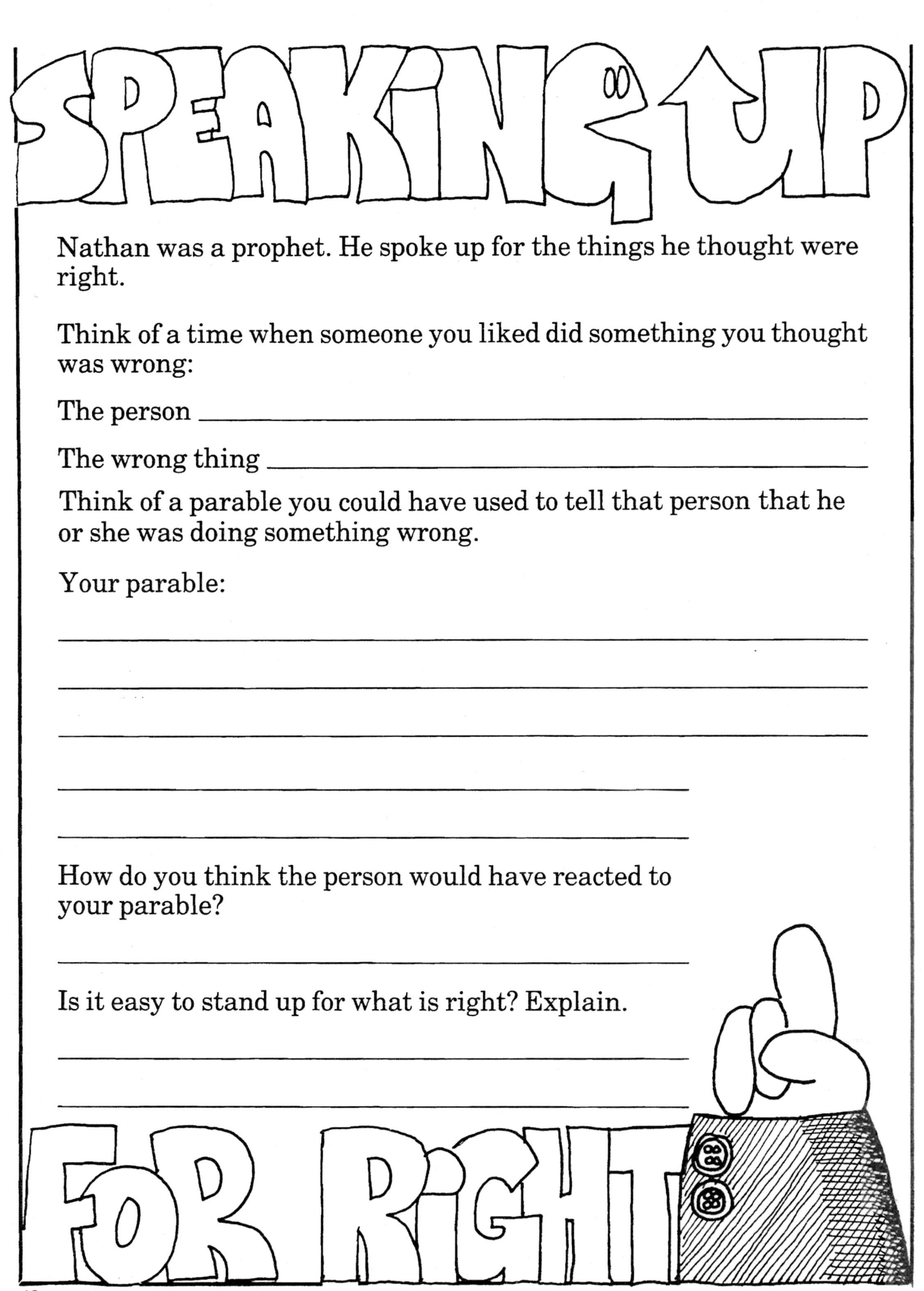

Nathan was a prophet. He spoke up for the things he thought were right.

Think of a time when someone you liked did something you thought was wrong:

The person _____

The wrong thing _____

Think of a parable you could have used to tell that person that he or she was doing something wrong.

Your parable:

_____
_____
_____
_____
_____

How do you think the person would have reacted to your parable?

_____

Is it easy to stand up for what is right? Explain.

_____
_____

FOR RIGHT

And all Israel...stood in awe of Solomon because they saw that the wisdom of God was in him...

I Kings 3:28

The Age of Solomon

King Solomon wasn't only a king. He was also a writer. He wrote throughout his life. At what stage of his life (youth, middle age, old age) do you think he made each of the following statements?

What good does a person get from all his/her work -
From all their labor under the sun?
One generation passes away and another generation comes
But the earth lasts forever.
The sun also rises and the sun goes down.

Ecclesiastes 1:4-5

Rise up my love my fair one and come away.
For the winter is past and the rain is over and gone;
The flowers appear on the earth and the time of singing is come.

Song of Songs 2:10-12

Hear, my son, the instruction of your father,
And don't forget your mother's teachings;
For they shall be a crown of goodness on your head,
and like chains around your neck.

Proverbs 1:3-4

SOLOMON'S CUBIT

The cubit used to be the basic unit of measure in biblical times. It was the distance between the elbow to the tip of the index finger. Find five adult males (the cubit was based on male measurements) and measure their cubits. Record their measurements in inches:

1. _____
2. _____
3. _____
4. _____
5. _____

_____ The total of the five

Divide your total by 5. This will give you an average length.

Our cubit is _____ inches long.

Noah's ark was 300 cubits long, 50 cubits wide, 30 cubits high. In feet and inches it would measure:

_____ long   _____ wide   _____ high

The Tabernacle was made up of planks which were 10 cubits high and 1½ cubits square. The Tabernacle had 20 planks standing on the long side. The short side was eight planks wide. In feet and inches, the Tabernacle would measure:

_____ long   _____ wide   _____ high

Solomon's Temple was 3 score cubits by 20 cubits and it was 30 cubits high. In feet and inches it would measure:

_____ long   _____ wide   _____ high

CHOOSING

Right after he became king, God asked Solomon what gift he would choose. Solomon chose wisdom. Number these gifts in the order you would choose them.

_____ wealth

_____ wisdom

_____ power

_____ artistic talent

_____ musical talent

_____ athletic ability

_____ good luck

_____ ability to read minds (ESP)

_____ great looks

_____ intelligence

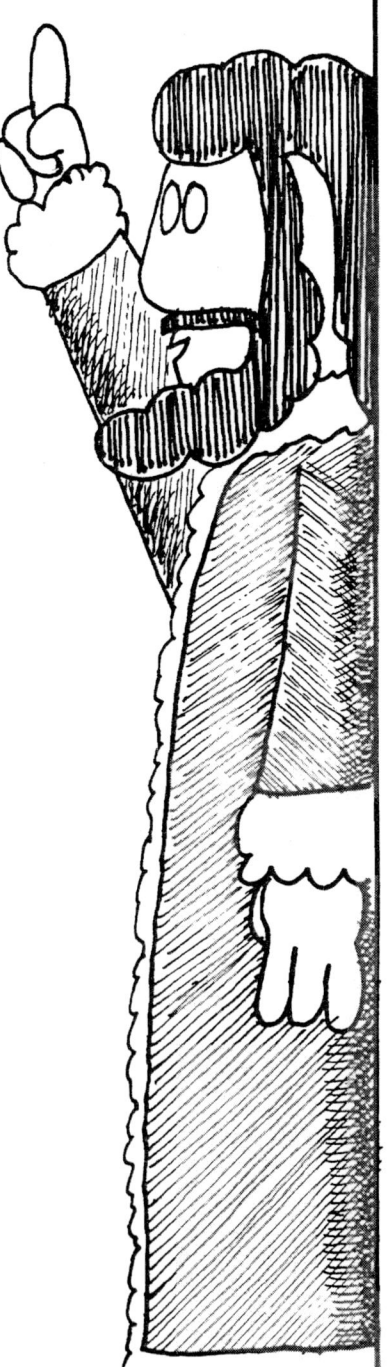

PLACING THE TEMPLE

The *midrash* tells us that King Solomon chose the location for the Temple because of an event that took place there between two brothers.

Archaeologists tell us that King Solomon chose the location for the Temple because it was the easiest spot to defend in the Jerusalem area.

What other good reasons could there be for choosing a location for worship?

1. _____

2. _____

3. _____

4. _____

53

According to the *midrash*, the following events all took place on the site where Solomon built The Temple:

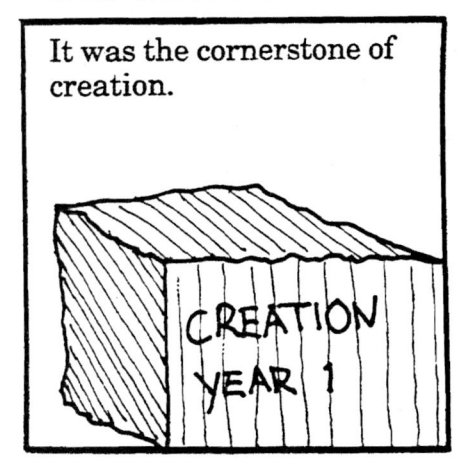

It was the cornerstone of creation.	It was the spot where Adam was created.	It was the place where Noah and family sacrificed after the flood.
It was the place where God told Abram to go.	It was the place where Abraham almost sacrificed Isaac.	It was where the end of the ladder in Jacob's dream rested.
It moved and provided the dry land for the crossing of the Sea of Reeds.	It was the source for the stone tablets on which the Ten Commandments were written.	It will be where redemption begins.

If all these things happened in this same spot, what kind of place would it be? _____

_____

Why do you think the Rabbis who wrote the *midrash* tried to connect these events to the place where Solomon built the Temple?

_____

MAKING YOUR CLASSROOM HOLY

Pretend you are a Rabbi who writes *midrashim.* Imagine three events which might have taken place where your classroom now is which would make it a holy, special, Jewish place. Draw and write about the three events.

ELIJAH

Elijah the Prophet, Elijah the Tishabite; come quickly in our time.
Come to us with Messiah, the son of David.

Traditional

THE ONCE AND FUTURE PROPHET

During his life, Elijah does all kinds of amazing things. When the time comes for his life to end, he doesn't die – but is carried off to heaven in a fiery chariot. Because he didn't die, the Rabbis believed that he was coming back to announce the end of this history and the beginning of *Olam HaBa* – The World to Come.

There are all kinds of legends that Elijah comes back and helps poor people who are in need.

Elijah is invited to every *seder*, to remind us that a time is coming when the world will be a place of peace and justice.

There is a chair for Elijah at every circumcision, because his being there reminds us of the hope for that child.

We welcome Elijah when we make Havdalah and end Shabbat, because that is a time when we hope for the Great Shabbat of the future.

In Hebrew the word for a tie is *Tay-ku*. It stands for the words:

תשבי יענה על השאלות והקשיות

It means, the Tishabite (Elijah) will answer all the questions and solve all the problems. The Rabbis really believed that when Elijah came again, history would end and the ideal world would begin.

1. What do you think "history" is?

2. When do you think history began?

3. Did anything happen before "history" began?

4. When do you think that history will end?

5. Will anything happen after history ends?

The Rabbis had their own view of history. They believed that history began with the creation of the world and that history will end at a time which they called "the end of days." That will be a time when all people will live in peace and will be unafraid. The Jewish people has a very special role in helping to bring about this ideal world.

CREATION

Creation is the beginning of time — a process which includes the origin of human beings.

THE HISTORY OF THE COVENANT

God and Abraham made a *brit*. This covenant said that God and the Jewish people have a special relationship, and also that they are partners in trying to perfect the world. This *brit* is continued by every generation of Abraham's family.

What will the world be like in 10 years?

What will the world be like in 50 years?

What will the world be like in 500 years?

The Rabbis believed that everything that happened to the Jewish People (both good and bad) was a step towards *Redemption* — the perfecting of the world. When the Jewish people lived by God's commandments, they improved the state of the world. When they were bad, the Rabbis believed that God helped them return to the right path. Eventually, when the job is complete, the world will be a place of freedom, peace, prosperity and all good things.

REVELATION

At Mt. Sinai, God gave Torah to Israel. At that moment in history, people received God's blueprint for the way they should live. At that moment, the Jewish people became a light to the nations.

THE MESSIAH

The Rabbis believed that the Messiah was a person, a descendant of King David, who would come and lead all people toward the final perfection of the world.

THE END OF DAYS

After the Messiah had completed his job, the world would be at peace and perfect. History would be over (no more need to struggle) and all people would be happy.

THE PROPHETS

Circle the statements about prophets you believe to be true:

1. Spoke the words of God
2. Lived the words of God
3. Predicted the future
4. Spoke out for truth and justice
5. Wrote words of poetry
6. Were filled with the words of God
7. Traveled in bands of prophets
8. Gave sermons
9. Had to be brave people
10. Were popular
11. Were unpopular
12. Were crazy people

The prophets delivered three kinds of messages:
1. Words of criticism (for things which are evil about individuals and society)
2. Words of prediction (what will happen because of the evil)
3. Words of comfort or hope for the future.

Which kind of message is reflected in each of the following prophetic statements?

Listen to this, you who devour the needy... saying, "If only the new moon were over, so that we could sell grain; the Sabbath, so that we could offer wheat for sale, using a measure that is too small, and a weight which is too big, tilting a dishonest scale.... We will buy the poor for silver, the needy for a pair of sandals."

Amos 8:4-6

In the days to come, the Mount of the Lord's House shall stand firm above the mountains... For instruction shall come forth from Zion, the word of the Lord from Jerusalem....And they shall beat their swords into plowshares, and their spears into pruning hooks. Nation shall not take up sword against nation; they shall never again know war....

Micah 4:1-3

Lo, I will send the prophet Elijah to you before the coming of the awesome, fearful day of the Lord. He shall reconcile parents with children and children with parents....

Malachi 3:23-24

The Lord will bring this charge
Against the elders and officers of His people:
"It is you who have ravaged the vineyard;
That which was stolen from the poor is in your houses.
How dare you crush My people
And grind the faces of the poor?" says my Lord God of Hosts.

         Isaiah 3:14

Thus said the Lord God to the land of Israel: "Doom Doom! is coming upon the four corners of the land...My anger is against you and will judge you according to your ways."

         Ezekiel 7:2-3

...at that time I will bring you home;
For I will make you renowned and famous
Among all the peoples of the earth,
When I restore your fortunes
Before their very eyes.

         Zephaniah 3:20

The days of punishment have come
For your heavy guilt;
The days of punishment have come –
Let Israel know it!

         Hosea 9:7

AMOS

I loathe, I spurn your festivals,
I am not appeased by your celebrations.
If you offer me sacrifices...
I will not accept them...
Spare Me the sound of your hymns,
And let Me not hear the music of your lutes.
But let justice well up like water and
Righteousness like an unfailing stream.

Amos 5:21-24

Amos was a simple man. He was a shepherd who also tended sycamore trees and who had little contact with formal religion. When the word of the Lord came to him, he left the small village of Tekoa, in the Southern Kingdom of Judah, where he was raised and went to the capital of the Northern Kingdom of Israel, Beth-El. There he stood on the Temple steps (probably on Yom Kippur) and delivered his message. It was a simple message, but an important one.

Amos said that God was angry with the way people were living. They treated each other poorly. They didn't follow God's laws and were worshiping other gods. He warned that if their behavior didn't improve, God would punish them.

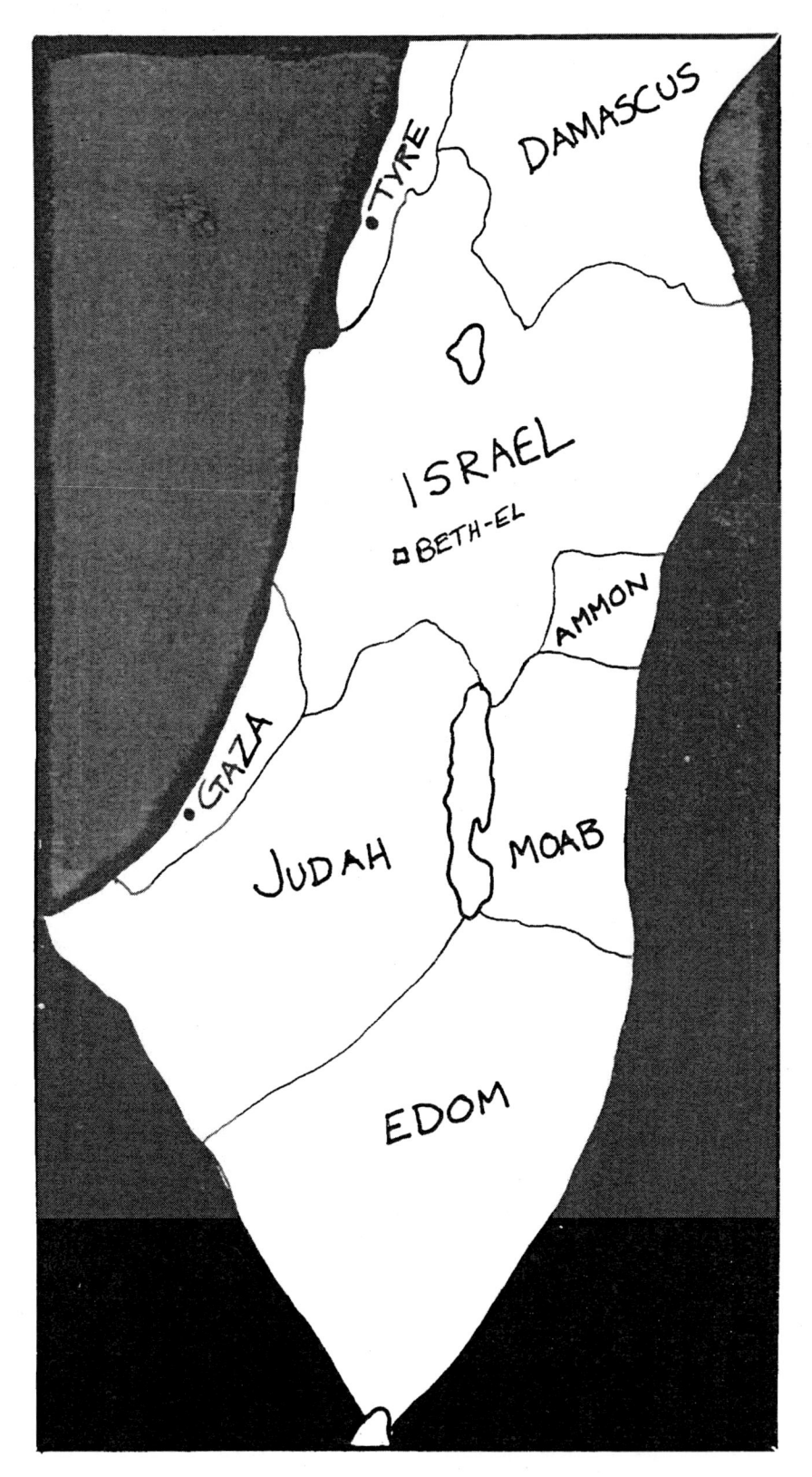

In his first major speech, Amos came to the Temple steps in Beth-El, the capital of Israel (a country which had split off from Judah). He gave a speech which promised that God would destroy a number of countries, most of which were enemies of the Jewish people. Number these countries on the map:

1. Damascus
2. Gaza
3. Tyre
4. Edom
5. Ammon
6. Moab
7. Judah
8. Israel

1. What kind of pattern do you see?

2. How do you think the people who heard Amos responded?

ORDERING JEWISH BEHAVIOR

Take this list of *mitzvot* and Jewish behaviors and put them in the order you think shows their importance. Number them from the most important to the least important. Then number them the way you think Amos would.

You　　Amos

_____　_____　Observing Shabbat

_____　_____　Not cursing the deaf or putting a stumbling block before the blind

_____　_____　Not worshiping other gods

_____　_____　Not eating pork

_____　_____　Giving *Keren Ami*

_____　_____　Fasting on Yom Kippur

_____　_____　Studying the Torah

_____　_____　Leaving the corners of your field for the poor, the widow and the orphan

_____　_____　Praying three times a day

_____　_____　Not cheating in business

HOSEA

I will betroth you to Me forever;
Yes, I will betroth you to Me in righteousness and justice, and in loving kindness and in compassion I will betroth you to Me in faithfulness; And you shall know the Lord.

                Hosea 2:21-22

Hosea compared the relationship between a husband and wife to the relationship between God and Israel. Just as a husband and wife are supposed to love each other – so, too, Israel and God had a special relationship. When Israel worshiped other gods and idols, they were "cheating" on their relationship with God.

Following God's orders, Hosea married a woman named Gomer and had three children with her. He named them: Jezreel - for the place where God will have Israel defeated, Lo-Ruhammah - meaning "I will not forgive," and Lo-Ammi - meaning "no longer my people." When Gomer cheated on him, he threw her out, just like he said God would do to Israel.

Hosea said that God said to Israel, "Return to me, and I will return to you." If Israel changed, then God would forgive the people, and the marriage between God and Israel could be saved.

RELATING TO GOD

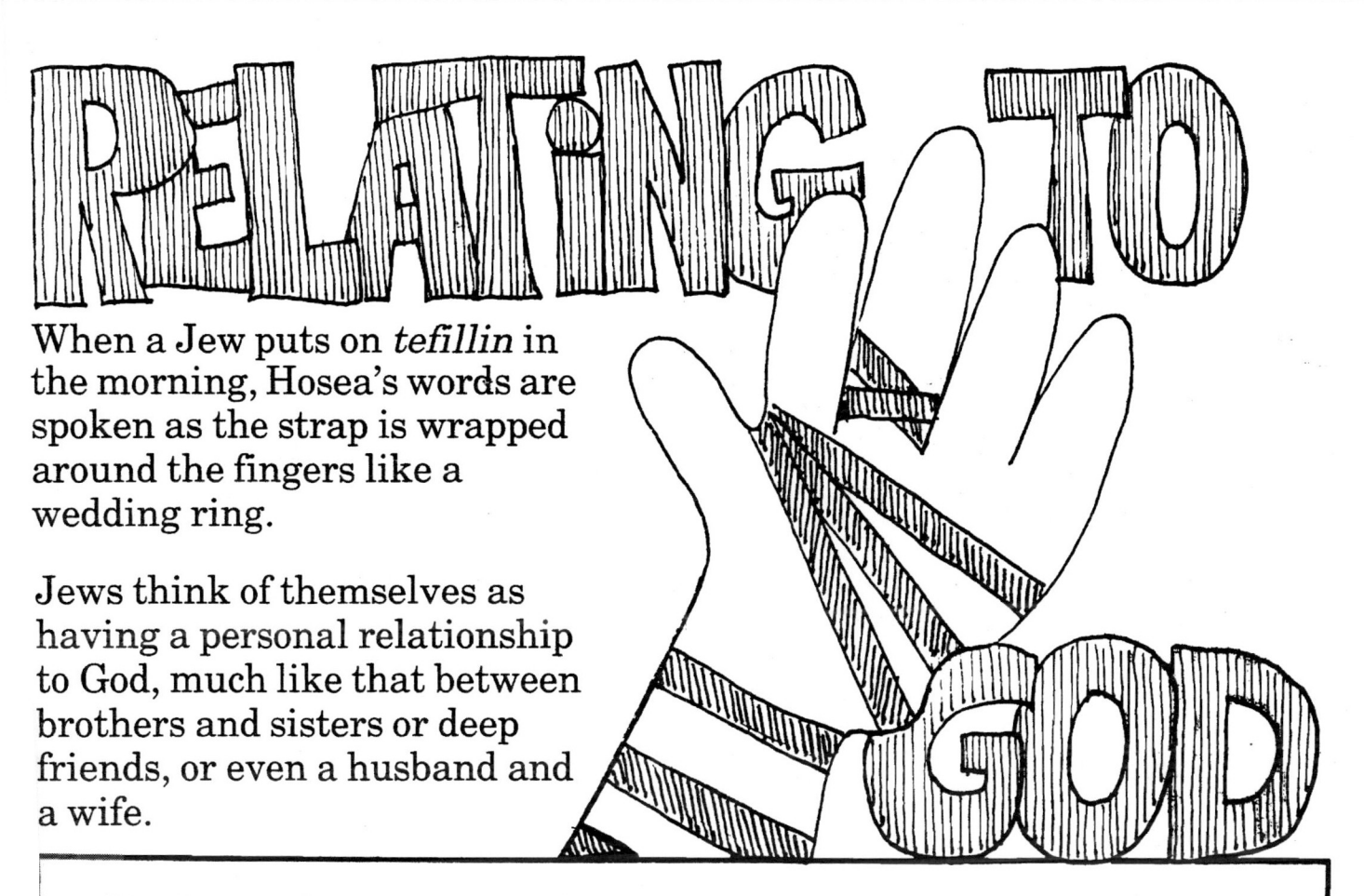

When a Jew puts on *tefillin* in the morning, Hosea's words are spoken as the strap is wrapped around the fingers like a wedding ring.

Jews think of themselves as having a personal relationship to God, much like that between brothers and sisters or deep friends, or even a husband and a wife.

All relationships require effort on our part if they are to remain close. List five things we can do to keep a close relationship to God:

1. _____
2. _____
3. _____
4. _____
5. _____

The quotation from Hosea on page 66 shows how God will keep his close relationship to us. In what ways does the world reflect God's righteousness, justice, lovingkindness, compassion, and faithfulness?

JEREMIAH

The word of the Lord came to me:
Before I created you in the womb,
I selected you, before you were
    born I consecrated you;
I appointed you a prophet...
I replied – Ah Lord God!
I don't know how to speak,
For I am still a boy.
And the Lord said to me:
Do not say, "I am still a boy,"
But go wherever I send you
And speak whatever I command you.

Jeremiah 1:4-7

Jeremiah was a prophet who didn't want to be a prophet. Sometimes we, too, are called upon to do things we don't really want to do. Circle the things below that you really don't want to do:

1. Go to religious school
2. Tell people that they have done wrong deeds
3. Listen to everything your parents tell you
4. Cheat or steal
5. Fast on Yom Kippur
6. Eat the bitter herbs on Pesach
7. Go to services
8. Give one tenth of your money to *Keren Ami* or *tzedakah*
9. Pick on, or make fun of, someone

Put a star by those which would be good for you to do even though you don't want to.

If you were a prophet today, list some things you would speak out against:

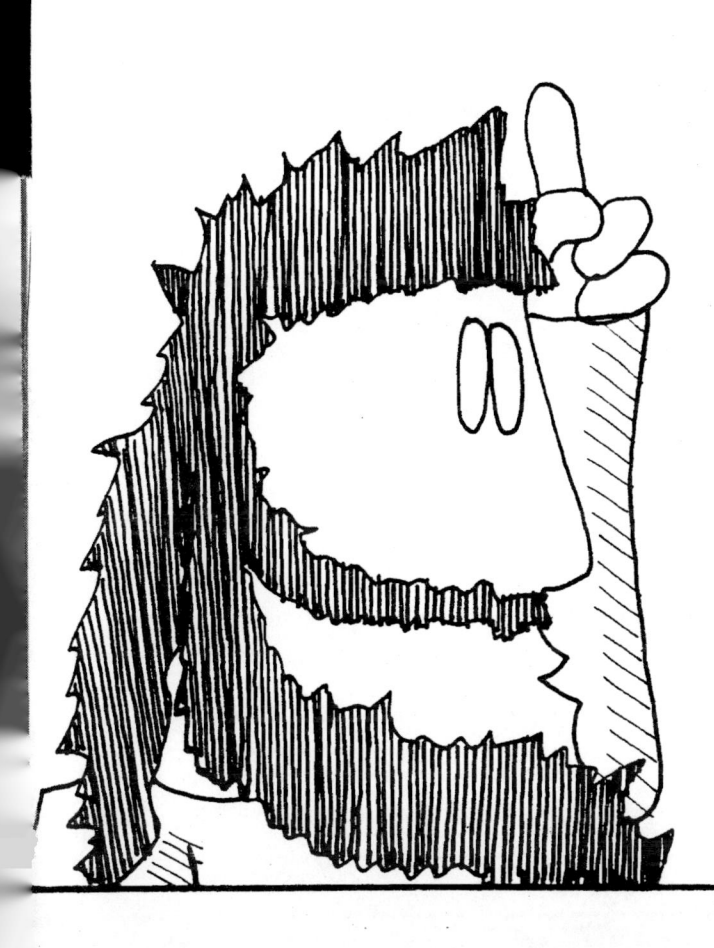

1. _____
2. _____
3. _____
4. _____
5. _____
6. _____
7. _____
8. _____
9. _____
10. _____

Jeremiah was a slightly different kind of prophet. He spoke about the same kinds of things that Amos and Hosea did, but he also spoke about politics. In his day, the Jewish people was caught between Egypt and Babylon. Some Jews wanted to join with Egypt and fight Babylon, but Jeremiah warned that God was against that. When the people didn't listen to Jeremiah and joined with Egypt, Babylon destroyed Israel. In 586 B.C.E. the entire nation was carried away as captives to Babylon.

When all of Israel was carried off as captives to Babylon, Jeremiah and a few other Jews escaped to Egypt. He sent a letter to the Jews of Babylon telling them that life should go on, that eventually God would forgive them and bring them back to their land.

Build houses and live in them. Plant gardens and eat their fruit; take wives and have children, and have your sons and daughters marry. Seek the peace of the city where God has caused you to be carried away captive, and pray unto the Lord for its peace, and you shall have peace in it.

Jeremiah

If you were going to tell Jews in your area to continue to live a normal Jewish life (just as Jeremiah told his people to carry on), what would you recommend they do?

1. _____
1. _____
2. _____
3. _____
4. _____
5. _____
6. _____
7. _____
8. _____

Esther,
Think not of yourself that you shall escape in the king's house, more than all the Jews. Because if you are quiet at this time, then help and deliverance will come to the Jews from another place, but you and your family will perish; and who knows if you came to your royal position for just such a time as this?
Mordecai
Esther 4:13-14
Go, gather together all the Jews in Shushan, and fast for me...I and my maidens will also fast, and so I will go in to the king.
Esther 4:16
ESTHER

TELLING THE TRUTH

Pick which of these you think is the REAL Queen Esther:

I didn't care much about my religion or my people when I married the king. But things happen... when Mordecai came to me, I really didn't want to tell the king that I was a Jew and risk everything. But sometimes a person has no choice. I discovered my Jewishness and came to love it.

I married the king because I thought that it might be good for our people. When the time came, I was scared. But I did what was needed and saved the Jewish people. After Haman was defeated, I used my position to help the Jewish people prosper.

I celebrated the holidays and the like, but when the chance came to marry the king, I wasn't going to let my religion stand in the way. However, when my people needed me, I had to help them out.

THE MISSING CHARACTER

Which of these characters seem to be missing from the Book of Esther?

When the Rabbis were putting the Bible together and deciding which books should be included, the Book of Esther gave them a hard time. They knew that it was an important story and that it was the basis of a holiday, but they didn't know if a book without the "missing character" could be in the Bible.

Do you think that a story which doesn't mention God should be in the Bible?

Some of the Rabbis argued that God was in the story. Where do you think these Rabbis found God in the Book of Esther?

If you were going to add God to the Esther story, at what point in the story would you have God get involved?

73

SUCCESS

START

MOVE AHEAD 5 SPACES

MOVE AHEAD 4 SPACES

MOVE AHEAD 3 SPACES

MOVE AHEAD 2 SPACES

MOVE AHEAD 1 SPACE

SUCCESS

FAILURE

OR

MOVE BACK 1 SPACE

MOVE BACK 2 SPACES

MOVE BACK 3 SPACES

MOVE BACK 4 SPACES

MOVE BACK 5 SPACES

FINISH

FAILURE

THIS GAME WAS DESIGNED BY CAROL ROSS

ALTERNATIVES WINTER 1978

Rules for Playing "Success and Failure"

1. This game is to be played in groups of four or less. So find a group.

2. In order to play, you will need a die and a marker for each player.

3. You will also need to make 4 Success Cards and 4 Failure Cards. Copy them from the bottom of this page, and put each group of cards in a stack with the text facing down.

4. The first person to reach the finish is the winner.

5. In order to move, a player rolls the die and moves. He/She follows the directions on the square on which he/she lands. If that square sends the player to a second square – he/she remains on the second square (but doesn't read or follow it's directions).

6. When you land on "Success," take a Success Card. When you land on "Failure," take a Failure Card with the same number as your Success Card.

Congratulations! You have earned an "A" in the high school class of your choice.	Sorry, but it's your own fault. Return your "A" and receive an "F" instead.
Congratulations! You have won $1,000 in cash.	Sorry, you couldn't handle the money. Return your $1,000 and pay 10% interest due for the loan.
Congratulations! You have won a new wardrobe. No $ limit.	Sorry your new wardrobe must be returned immediately. Pay store for any clothes you have already worn.
Congratulations! You have won free admission to 100 movies of your choice.	Cancel movie offer.

There was a man in the land of Uz, whose name was Job, and that man was wholehearted and upright, and one who feared God and stayed away from evil.

Job 1:1

GOD-TALK

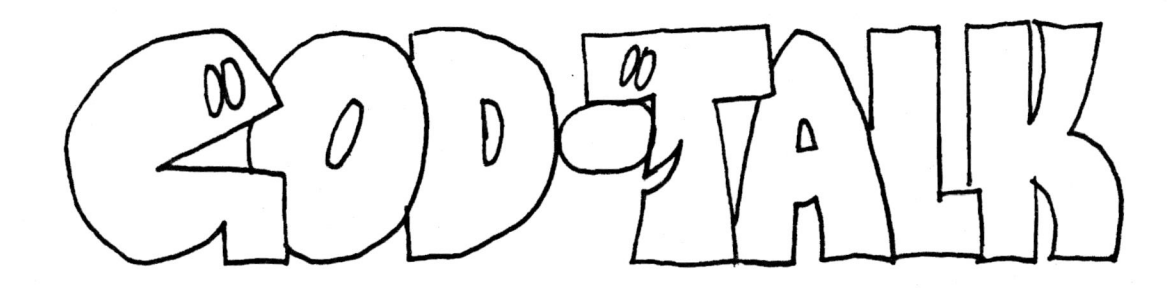

The book of Job asks one of the hardest questions about God. Often our first thoughts about God lead us to believe that God rewards people for good actions and punishes people for bad actions. That would mean that good people should have a happy life, and that bad people should have an unhappy life.

Can you give some examples of times when this is true?

Can you give some examples of times when this doesn't seem to be true?

Each of the following ideas about God is a way of explaining how people can do good, and yet still seem to have unhappy lives. Explain how each of these ideas allows God to be *fair* to good people.

1. Life after death (with heaven and hell)

2. Reincarnation (being reborn as another person)

3. Children being rewarded or punished for their parents' actions.

How do *you* explain why God lets good people suffer?

JEWISH LEADERS

PATRIARCHS AND MATRIARCHS

PROPHETS

PRIESTS

JUDGES

KINGS

TYPES OF LEADERS

Put an X in the box if the statement is true for leaders in that category.	Patriarchs Matriarchs	Prophets	Judges	Priests	Kings
1. Talked with God					
2. Led worship					
3. Judged people					
4. Led battles					
5. Was related to Abraham					
6. Was related to Aaron					
7. Was related to David					
8. Taught Torah					
9. Was anointed					
10. Led by strong personality					

Abraham					
Sarah					
Isaac					
Rachel					
Jacob					
Leah					
Rebekah					
Joseph					
Moses					
Aaron					
Miriam					
Joshua					
Deborah					
Samson					
Samuel					
Ruth					
Saul					
David					
Nathan					
Solomon					
Amos					
Jeremiah					
Hosea					
Esther					
Job					

JEWISH LEADERSHIP TEST

Give yourself five points for each of these things you can do. Give yourself ten points for each of these things you could teach to a friend.

_____ Read Hebrew
_____ Tell Bible stories
_____ Dance an Israeli dance
_____ Sing an Israeli song
_____ Find a Jewish organization to help with a problem
_____ Help lead a worship service
_____ Make a kosher meal
_____ List ten acts of *tzedakah*
_____ Explain most Jewish holidays
_____ Celebrate the customs of most Jewish holidays
_____ Name more than five Jewish places near where you live
_____ Name 20 Jewish books
_____ Open a Bible to Exodus 20:16
_____ List six Jewish values
_____ Locate six places on a blank map of Israel
_____ Put up a *mezzuzah*
_____ List ten things which make a home Jewish
_____ Speak Hebrew
_____ Tell your family history
_____ Lead the dinner table service on Erev Shabbat

My score is _____ . I think a passing score is _____ .
Which of the above skills do you think is most important?
Underline those things you think Moses could have done.
Which of these skills would you most like to learn?